DR. GEORGINA TRACY

high
CALORIE
SMOOTHIES
FOR WEIGHT GAIN

WITH
28-day
exercise plan

high

CALORIE

SMOOTHIES

FOR WEIGHT GAIN

The Most Powerful High Calorie Blends to Help Boost Your Weight Gain Process.

DR. GEORGINA TRACY

Contents

Introduction

Dear reader,

Are you tired of feeling insecure about your body? Do you want to gain weight in a healthy way without resorting to unhealthy junk food? If yes, then welcome to my high-calorie smoothies for weight gain book. My name is Dr. Georgina Tracy, and I am a certified nutritionist who has helped countless people achieve their weight gain goals through healthy, delicious smoothies.

Many people struggle with weight gain, and this can be especially challenging for adult men and women. Society often puts pressure on us to look a certain way, which can lead to unhealthy habits and low self-esteem. But it doesn't have to be that way. With the right tools and mindset, you can embrace your journey to healthy weight gain and feel confident in your own skin.

In this book, I will share with you my favorite high-calorie smoothie recipes that are not only delicious but also packed with nutrients. These smoothies are designed to help you gain weight in a healthy and sustainable way. Each recipe is carefully crafted to provide you with the essential macronutrients needed for weight gain - protein, carbohydrates, and healthy fats.

But it's not just about the ingredients. I will also share with you tips on how to make your smoothies even more enjoyable, so you look forward to drinking them every day. Plus, I will show you how to combine your smoothies with a balanced diet and exercise plan to achieve optimal results.

So, are you ready to embark on this journey with me? Let's embrace our bodies and work towards healthy weight gain, one delicious smoothie at a time.

Tips for Making Delicious High-Calorie Smoothies

Making delicious high-calorie smoothies can be both fun and rewarding. It is an opportunity to be creative and experiment with different flavors and ingredients to find what works best for your taste buds. In this chapter, I'll share with you some tips for making delicious high-calorie smoothies.

How to Choose the Best Ingredients

The best way to ensure that your smoothies taste amazing is to choose high-quality ingredients. Here are some tips on how to choose the best ingredients for your high-calorie smoothies:

- **Choose fresh, ripe fruits and vegetables:** Using fresh, ripe fruits and vegetables will give your smoothies the best flavor and nutritional value.

- **Use frozen fruits and vegetables**: Frozen fruits and vegetables are a great way to add creaminess and texture to your smoothies.

- **Choose high-quality protein powders:** Look for protein powders that are made from high-quality ingredients and have a high protein content.
- **Use healthy fats:** Adding healthy fats like avocado, nuts, and seeds can help to make your smoothies more filling and satisfying.

Kitchen Tools and Techniques

Using the right kitchen tools and techniques can also help to make your high-calorie smoothies taste amazing. Here are some tips:

- **Use a high-powered blender:** A high-powered blender can help to blend your smoothie ingredients into a creamy, smooth consistency.
- **Add liquid ingredients first:** Adding liquid ingredients like milk or juice to your blender first can help to get the blending process started.
- **Blend for at least 30 seconds:** To ensure that your smoothie is smooth and creamy, blend for at least 30 seconds.

You'll also need a sharp knife, a cutting board, and measuring cups and spoons. When blending, start with the liquid ingredients and then add the solids slowly, pulsing the blender as you go.

Essential Ingredients for High-Calorie Smoothies

There are certain ingredients that are essential for making high-calorie smoothies. Here are some of the key ingredients to include:

- **Protein powder:** Protein powder is an easy way to add extra protein and calories to your smoothies.
- **Nut butter:** Nut butter is a great way to add healthy fats and calories to your smoothies.
- **Milk or yogurt:** Adding milk or yogurt to your smoothies can help to make them creamy and delicious.
- **Fruit and vegetables:** Fruits and vegetables are an important source of vitamins, minerals, and fiber.

By following these tips and using the right ingredients, you can make delicious high-calorie smoothies that will help you achieve your weight gain goals.

The Most Powerful High-Calorie Smoothies for Weight Gain

Breakfast Smoothies for High-Calorie Weight Gain

CHOCOLATE PEANUT BUTTER BANANA SMOOTHIE

This smoothie is a delicious and healthy way to gain weight. It's packed with protein and healthy fats, making it perfect for anyone looking to add some extra calories to their diet. Plus, it's rich, creamy, and tastes like dessert!

This smoothie is high in protein, healthy fats, and carbs, making it perfect for post-workout recovery or as a meal replacement. The peanut butter adds healthy fats, while the banana provides a good source of carbs and potassium.

Ingredients:

- 1 ripe banana

- 1 scoop chocolate protein powder
- 1 tablespoon natural peanut butter
- 1 cup unsweetened almond milk
- 1/2 cup ice

Directions:

- Add all ingredients to a blender.
- Blend until smooth and creamy.
- Pour into a glass and enjoy!

Nutritional information:

- Calories: 360
- Protein: 25g
- Fat: 15g
- Carbs: 36g

BLUEBERRY ALMOND BUTTER SMOOTHIE

This smoothie is a great way to pack in some extra calories and nutrition. It's loaded with healthy fats, protein, and antioxidants from the blueberries. Plus, it's creamy, delicious, and easy to make.

This smoothie is high in protein and healthy fats, making it perfect for anyone looking to gain weight or maintain muscle mass. The blueberries provide antioxidants, which can help support overall health and wellbeing.

Ingredients:

- 1/2 cup frozen blueberries
- 1 tablespoon almond butter
- 1 scoop vanilla protein powder
- 1 cup unsweetened almond milk
- 1/2 cup ice

Directions:

- Add all ingredients to a blender.
- Blend until smooth and creamy.
- Pour into a glass and enjoy!

Nutritional information:

- Calories: 320
- Protein: 22g
- Fat: 12g
- Carbs: 32g

STRAWBERRY MANGO COCONUT SMOOTHIE

This smoothie is a tropical treat that's perfect for gaining weight. It's loaded with healthy fats, carbs, and antioxidants, making it a great option for anyone looking to support their overall health and wellbeing.

This smoothie is high in healthy fats, carbs, and antioxidants, making it a great option for anyone looking to gain weight and support their overall health. The strawberries and mango provide a good source of vitamin C, which can help support immune function.

Ingredients:

- 1/2 cup frozen mango
- 1/2 cup frozen strawberries
- 1 scoop vanilla protein powder
- 1 tablespoon coconut oil
- 1 cup unsweetened coconut milk
- 1/2 cup ice

Directions:

- Add all ingredients to a blender.
- Blend until smooth and creamy.
- Pour into a glass and enjoy!

Nutritional information:

- Calories: 370
- Protein: 23g
- Fat: 17g
- Carbs: 34g

PEACH PIE SMOOTHIE

This delicious smoothie is a perfect addition to your weight gain diet plan. The ingredients are chosen carefully to ensure that the smoothie is high in calories, healthy fats, and protein.

Peaches are a great source of dietary fiber and vitamins A and C, while Greek yogurt provides a healthy dose of protein, calcium, and probiotics. The almond butter is a healthy fat that helps to keep you feeling full for longer periods of time.

Ingredients:

- 2 ripe peaches, pitted and chopped
- 1 cup unsweetened vanilla almond milk
- 1/2 cup plain Greek yogurt
- 1 tablespoon almond butter
- 1 tablespoon honey
- 1/4 teaspoon ground cinnamon

- 1/4 teaspoon vanilla extract
- 1 cup ice cubes

Directions:

- Add all ingredients to a blender and blend until smooth.
- Pour into a glass and enjoy immediately.

Nutritional Information:

- Calories: 410
- Protein: 16g
- Fat: 17g
- Carbohydrates: 53g
- Fiber: 6g
- Sugar: 41g

Post-Workout Smoothies for High-Calorie Weight Gain

BANANA NUTELLA SMOOTHIE

This high-calorie smoothie is a delicious blend of sweet bananas and rich Nutella, making it a perfect choice for anyone looking to gain weight. Bananas are a great source of carbohydrates, while Nutella provides healthy fats, and protein-rich Greek yogurt adds a creamy texture.

Ingredients:

- 2 ripe bananas
- 2 tbsp Nutella
- 1/2 cup Greek yogurt
- 1/2 cup whole milk
- 1 tbsp honey
- 1/2 tsp vanilla extract
- 1 cup ice

Directions:

- Add all ingredients to a blender and blend until smooth.
- Pour into a glass and enjoy!
- Nutritional information (per serving):

- Calories: 450
- Protein: 15g
- Carbohydrates: 60g
- Fat: 18g

CHOCOLATE AVOCADO SMOOTHIE

Avocado is a great ingredient for weight gain smoothies as it is high in healthy fats and calories. This smoothie also includes chocolate protein powder for an extra protein boost, making it perfect for post-workout recovery.

Ingredients:

- 1 ripe avocado
- 1 scoop chocolate protein powder
- 1/2 cup almond milk
- 1/2 cup ice
- 1 tbsp honey
- 1/2 tsp vanilla extract

Directions:

- Add all ingredients to a blender and blend until smooth.
- Pour into a glass and enjoy!

Nutritional information (per serving):

- Calories: 400
- Protein: 30g
- Carbohydrates: 20g
- Fat: 25g

MANGO TURMERIC SMOOTHIE

This high-calorie smoothie is a great option for those looking to reduce inflammation and boost their immune system. Mangoes are high in calories and antioxidants, while turmeric adds anti-inflammatory benefits.

Ingredients:

- 1 ripe mango
- 1/2 cup Greek yogurt
- 1/2 cup whole milk
- 1/2 tsp turmeric
- 1 tbsp honey
- 1/2 tsp vanilla extract
- 1 cup ice

Directions:

- Add all ingredients to a blender and blend until smooth.

- Pour into a glass and enjoy!

Nutritional information (per serving):

- Calories: 380

- Protein: 15g

- Carbohydrates: 50g

- Fat: 15g

TROPICAL GREEN SMOOTHIE

This high-calorie smoothie is packed with nutrient-dense ingredients like spinach and pineapple, making it a great option for those looking to boost their overall health and gain weight. The addition of coconut milk provides healthy fats and calories.

Ingredients:

- 1 cup fresh spinach

- 1 cup frozen pineapple chunks

- 1/2 cup coconut milk

- 1/2 cup Greek yogurt

- 1 tbsp honey

- 1/2 tsp vanilla extract

Directions:

- Add all ingredients to a blender and blend until smooth.
- Pour into a glass and enjoy!

Nutritional information (per serving):

- Calories: 350
- Protein: 15g
- Carbohydrates: 40g
- Fat: 18g

Dessert-Inspired Smoothies for High-Calorie Weight Gain

MINT CHOCOLATE CHIP SMOOTHIE

This high-calorie smoothie is not only delicious but also packed with nutrients to help you gain weight. The combination of mint and chocolate chips creates a heavenly taste that will keep you wanting more. It's perfect for a quick breakfast or post-workout snack.

This smoothie is high in calories, healthy fats, and protein, which are all essential for weight gain. The spinach in this smoothie provides iron which is important for building muscles and increasing metabolism.

Ingredients:

- 2 frozen bananas
- 1/2 cup spinach
- 1/4 cup mint leaves
- 1/2 avocado
- 1 scoop chocolate protein powder
- 1/4 cup chocolate chips
- 1 cup almond milk

Directions:

- Add all the ingredients in a blender.
- Blend until smooth.
- Pour into a glass and enjoy!

Nutritional Information:

- Calories: 563
- Protein: 28g
- Fat: 24g
- Carbohydrates: 72g

VANILLA CHAI SMOOTHIE

This smoothie is a perfect way to start your day on a high note. It has a sweet, creamy taste that will keep you energized throughout the day. The combination of vanilla and chai spices gives it a unique flavor that is hard to resist.

This smoothie is high in calories, healthy fats, and protein, which are all essential for weight gain. The chai spices in this smoothie help boost metabolism and aid digestion.

Ingredients:

- 2 frozen bananas
- 1/2 cup oats
- 1/2 cup plain Greek yogurt
- 1 scoop vanilla protein powder
- 1 tsp cinnamon
- 1 tsp ground ginger
- 1/2 tsp cardamom
- 1/2 tsp nutmeg
- 1 cup almond milk

Directions:

- Add all the ingredients in a blender.
- Blend until smooth.

- Pour into a glass and enjoy!

Nutritional Information:

- Calories: 543
- Protein: 40g
- Fat: 9g
- Carbohydrates: 81g

CINNAMON ROLL SMOOTHIE

This high-calorie smoothie tastes like a cinnamon roll in a glass. It's sweet, creamy, and has a hint of cinnamon that will satisfy your sweet tooth. It's perfect for those who love cinnamon rolls but want to stick to a healthy diet.

This smoothie is high in calories, protein, and healthy fats, which are all essential for weight gain. The cinnamon in this smoothie helps to regulate blood sugar levels, and the almond butter is a great source of healthy fats.

Ingredients:

- 2 frozen bananas
- 1/2 cup oats

- 1 tbsp almond butter
- 1 scoop vanilla protein powder
- 1 tsp cinnamon
- 1/2 tsp vanilla extract
- 1 cup almond milk

Directions:

- Add all the ingredients in a blender.
- Blend until smooth.
- Pour into a glass and enjoy!

Nutritional Information:

- Calories: 569
- Protein: 39g
- Fat: 19g
- Carbohydrates: 70g

OATMEAL COOKIE SMOOTHIE

This high-calorie smoothie is packed with essential nutrients that can help women gain weight healthily. The oats in this smoothie provide a slow-releasing source of energy, which can keep you feeling full and satisfied for longer periods. Also, the protein in the

Greek yogurt and almond butter will help to repair muscle tissue after workouts, while the bananas provide a good source of natural sugars to fuel your body.

Ingredients:

- 1 ripe banana
- 1/2 cup rolled oats
- 1 cup unsweetened vanilla almond milk
- 1 tablespoon almond butter
- 1 tablespoon honey
- 1/4 teaspoon ground cinnamon
- 1/4 teaspoon vanilla extract
- 1 scoop vanilla protein powder (optional)

Directions:

- In a blender, add the rolled oats and blend until they form a fine powder.
- Add the banana, almond milk, almond butter, honey, cinnamon, vanilla extract, and protein powder (if using) to the blender.
- Blend all ingredients until smooth and creamy.
- Pour into a glass and enjoy!

Nutritional Information (per serving):

- Calories: 405

- Protein: 16g
- Fat: 12g
- Carbohydrates: 64g
- Fiber: 8g

WITH SMOOTHIES SPECIFICALLY RECOMMENDED FOR FEMALE WEIGHT GAIN. CLICK HERE TO GET ON AMAZON NOW!

Nut-Free High-Calorie Smoothies for Weight Gain

RASPBERRY WHITE CHOCOLATE SMOOTHIE

This Raspberry White Chocolate Smoothie is an indulgent treat that also helps you pack on those extra calories. The combination of raspberries and white chocolate creates a deliciously sweet and tart flavor that is perfect for satisfying your cravings.

Ingredients:

- 1 cup frozen raspberries
- 1 cup vanilla yogurt
- 1/2 cup milk
- 1/4 cup white chocolate chips
- 1 tablespoon honey
- 1 tablespoon chia seeds

Directions:

- In a blender, combine the frozen raspberries, vanilla yogurt, milk, white chocolate chips, honey, and chia seeds.
- Blend until smooth and creamy, adding more milk if needed to reach your desired consistency.
- Pour into a glass and enjoy!

Nutritional Information:

- Calories: 535
- Protein: 16g
- Fat: 20g
- Carbohydrates: 76g
- Fiber: 12g

COCONUT PINEAPPLE SMOOTHIE

This Coconut Pineapple Smoothie is a tropical delight that will transport you straight to the beach. The combination of coconut and pineapple creates a refreshing and creamy flavor that is perfect for any time of day.

Ingredients:

- 1 cup frozen pineapple chunks
- 1 cup coconut milk
- 1/2 cup vanilla yogurt
- 1 tablespoon honey
- 1 tablespoon coconut oil

Directions:

- In a blender, combine the frozen pineapple chunks, coconut milk, vanilla yogurt, honey, and coconut oil.

- Blend until smooth and creamy, adding more coconut milk if needed to reach your desired consistency.
- Pour into a glass and enjoy!

Nutritional Information:

- Calories: 440
- Protein: 5g
- Fat: 26g
- Carbohydrates: 48g
- Fiber: 4g

CHOCOLATE CHERRY SMOOTHIE

This Chocolate Cherry Smoothie is a decadent treat that is perfect for any chocolate lover. The combination of chocolate and cherries creates a rich and indulgent flavor that is sure to satisfy your cravings.

Ingredients:

- 1 cup frozen cherries
- 1 cup chocolate almond milk

- 1/2 cup vanilla yogurt
- 1 tablespoon honey
- 1 tablespoon almond butter

Directions:

- In a blender, combine the frozen cherries, chocolate almond milk, vanilla yogurt, honey, and almond butter.
- Blend until smooth and creamy, adding more almond milk if needed to reach your desired consistency.
- Pour into a glass and enjoy!

Nutritional Information:

- Calories: 430
- Protein: 11g
- Fat: 18g
- Carbohydrates: 61g
- Fiber: 6g

PEACH COBBLER SMOOTHIE

This Peach Cobbler Smoothie is a deliciously sweet and satisfying way to indulge your sweet tooth while packing on those extra calories. The combination of peaches and cinnamon creates a warm and comforting flavor that is perfect for any time of day.

Ingredients:

- 1 cup frozen peaches
- 1 cup vanilla almond milk
- 1/2 cup vanilla yogurt
- 1 tablespoon honey
- 1 teaspoon cinnamon

Directions:

- In a blender, combine the frozen peaches, vanilla almond milk, vanilla yogurt, honey, and cinnamon.
- Blend until smooth and creamy, adding more almond milk if needed to reach your desired consistency.
- Pour into a glass and enjoy!

Nutritional Information:

- Calories: 380
- Protein: 9g
- Fat: 7g
- Carbohydrates: 71g
- Fiber: 7g

WEIGHT

Superfood-Boosted Smoothies for High-Calorie Weight Gain

ACAI BERRY SUPERFOOD SMOOTHIE

This smoothie is packed with antioxidants and essential nutrients that help to support weight gain. It is made with acai berries, which are known for their high levels of antioxidants, fiber, and healthy fats. The smoothie also contains bananas and almond milk, which are both excellent sources of calories and nutrients that can help with weight gain.

Ingredients:

- 1 cup frozen acai berries
- 1 banana
- 1 cup unsweetened almond milk
- 1 tablespoon honey (optional)

Directions:

- Add the frozen acai berries, banana, almond milk, and honey (if using) to a blender.
- Blend until smooth and creamy.
- Pour into a glass and enjoy!

Nutritional Information:

- Calories: 328
- Protein: 4g
- Carbohydrates: 52g
- Fat: 12g
- Fiber: 9g

SPIRULINA GREEN SMOOTHIE

This smoothie is perfect for weight gain as it contains spirulina, which is a nutrient-dense superfood that is rich in protein, vitamins, and minerals. The smoothie also contains spinach, which is a great source of iron, and bananas, which are high in calories and nutrients.

Ingredients:

- 1 banana
- 1 cup spinach
- 1 cup unsweetened almond milk
- 1 teaspoon spirulina powder
- 1 tablespoon honey (optional)

Directions:

- Add the banana, spinach, almond milk, spirulina powder, and honey (if using) to a blender.
- Blend until smooth and creamy.
- Pour into a glass and enjoy!

Nutritional Information:

- Calories: 257
- Protein: 6g
- Carbohydrates: 43g
- Fat: 8g
- Fiber: 7g

GOJI BERRY BANANA SMOOTHIE

This smoothie is a delicious way to add calories and nutrients to your diet. It is made with goji berries, which are high in fiber and antioxidants, and bananas, which are a great source of calories and nutrients.

Ingredients:

- 1 banana

- 1/2 cup frozen goji berries
- 1 cup unsweetened almond milk
- 1 tablespoon honey (optional)

Directions:

- Add the banana, goji berries, almond milk, and honey (if using) to a blender.
- Blend until smooth and creamy.
- Pour into a glass and enjoy!

Nutritional Information:

- Calories: 237
- Protein: 4g
- Carbohydrates: 41g
- Fat: 7g
- Fiber: 8g

MACA CACAO SMOOTHIE

This smoothie is a great way to boost your energy levels and support healthy weight gain. It is made with maca powder, which is known for its ability to increase energy, and cacao powder, which is rich in antioxidants and magnesium.

Ingredients:

- 1 banana
- 1 tablespoon maca powder
- 1 tablespoon cacao powder
- 1 cup unsweetened almond milk
- 1 tablespoon honey (optional)

Directions:

- Add the banana, maca powder, cacao powder, almond milk, and honey (if using) to a blender.
- Blend until smooth and creamy.
- Pour into a glass and enjoy!

Nutritional Information:

- Calories: 269
- Protein: 5g
- Carbohydrates: 44g
- Fat: 9g
- Fiber: 7g

Meal Replacement Smoothies for High-Calorie Weight Gain

BLUEBERRY MUFFIN SMOOTHIE

This Blueberry Muffin Smoothie is perfect for anyone looking to gain weight without sacrificing taste. It's packed with healthy fats, protein, and carbohydrates to give your body the fuel it needs to build muscle and gain weight.

Ingredients:

- 1 cup frozen blueberries
- 1/2 cup Greek yogurt
- 1/2 cup milk
- 1/4 cup oats
- 1 tbsp almond butter
- 1 tbsp honey
- 1 tsp vanilla extract
- 1/4 tsp cinnamon

Directions:

- Add all ingredients to a blender and blend until smooth.
- Pour into a glass and enjoy!

Nutritional Information (per serving):

- Calories: 350
- Protein: 15g
- Carbohydrates: 48g
- Fat: 12g
- Fiber: 6g

BANANA BREAD SMOOTHIE

This Banana Bread Smoothie is a delicious way to pack in the calories you need for weight gain. It's loaded with healthy fats, protein, and carbs, making it the perfect breakfast or post-workout snack.

Ingredients:

- 2 ripe bananas
- 1/2 cup Greek yogurt
- 1/2 cup milk
- 1/4 cup oats
- 1 tbsp almond butter
- 1 tbsp honey
- 1 tsp vanilla extract

- 1/4 tsp nutmeg
- 1/4 tsp cinnamon

Directions:

- Add all ingredients to a blender and blend until smooth.
- Pour into a glass and enjoy!

Nutritional Information (per serving):

- Calories: 400
- Protein: 15g
- Carbohydrates: 62g
- Fat: 11g
- Fiber: 7g

CHOCOLATE BERRY SMOOTHIE

This Chocolate Berry Smoothie is a tasty and satisfying way to pack in the calories for weight gain. It's loaded with healthy fats, protein, and carbs, and the chocolate flavor makes it feel like a treat!

Ingredients:

- 1 cup mixed berries (fresh or frozen)
- 1/2 cup Greek yogurt

- 1/2 cup milk

- 1 tbsp almond butter

- 1 tbsp cocoa powder

- 1 tbsp honey

- 1 tsp vanilla extract

Directions:

- Add all ingredients to a blender and blend until smooth.

- Pour into a glass and enjoy!

Nutritional Information (per serving):

- Calories: 375

- Protein: 17g

- Carbohydrates: 45g

- Fat: 15g

- Fiber: 8g

PB&J SMOOTHIE

This PB&J Smoothie is a delicious and fun way to get the calories you need for weight gain. It's packed with healthy fats, protein, and carbs, and the peanut butter and jelly flavors will bring you right back to childhood.

Ingredients:

- 1/2 cup frozen strawberries
- 1/2 cup frozen raspberries
- 1/2 cup milk
- 1/2 cup Greek yogurt
- 2 tbsp peanut butter
- 1 tbsp honey
- 1 tsp vanilla extract

Directions:

- Add all ingredients to a blender and blend until smooth.
- Pour into a glass and enjoy!

Nutritional Information (per serving):

- Calories: 425
- Protein: 23g
- Carbohydrates: 44g
- Fat: 19g
- Fiber: 8g

INTERESTED? CLICK HERE TO GET IT ON AMAZON NOW!

28-Day Exercise Plan for

Weight Gain.

Exercise Plan for Men

For the next 30 days, I recommend following this workout plan for optimal weight gain:

WEEK 1: FOCUS ON STRENGTH TRAINING

- Day 1: Upper Body Strength Training (chest, back, arms, and shoulders)
- Day 2: Lower Body Strength Training (legs and glutes)
- Day 3: Rest
- Day 4: Upper Body Strength Training
- Day 5: Lower Body Strength Training
- Day 6: Rest
- Day 7: Rest

WEEK 2: HIGH-INTENSITY INTERVAL TRAINING (HIIT)

- Day 1: 20 minutes of HIIT on a stationary bike or treadmill
- Day 2: 20 minutes of HIIT using bodyweight exercises (burpees, jumping jacks, etc.)
- Day 3: Rest
- Day 4: 20 minutes of HIIT on a stair climber or rowing machine
- Day 5: 20 minutes of HIIT using dumbbells or resistance bands
- Day 6: Rest
- Day 7: Rest

WEEK 3: CARDIOVASCULAR ENDURANCE TRAINING

- Day 1: 30 minutes of running or jogging
- Day 2: 30 minutes of cycling
- Day 3: Rest
- Day 4: 30 minutes of swimming or using an elliptical machine
- Day 5: 30 minutes of jump rope or aerobic dance
- Day 6: Rest
- Day 7: Rest

WEEK 4: CIRCUIT TRAINING

- Day 1: Full-body circuit training using dumbbells or resistance bands

- Day 2: Rest
- Day 3: Full-body circuit training using bodyweight exercises
- Day 4: Rest
- Day 5: Full-body circuit training using kettlebells or sandbags
- Day 6: Rest
- Day 7: Rest

For Women

WEEK 1:

- Day 1: 20-minute walk + 10 minutes of resistance band exercises
- Day 2: Rest
- Day 3: 25-minute jog + 10 minutes of bodyweight exercises
- Day 4: 30-minute yoga session
- Day 5: Rest
- Day 6: 20-minute walk + 10 minutes of resistance band exercises
- Day 7: 25-minute jog + 10 minutes of bodyweight exercises

WEEK 2:

- Day 8: Rest

- Day 9: 25-minute jog + 10 minutes of resistance band exercises
- Day 10: 30-minute yoga session
- Day 11: 25-minute swim + 10 minutes of bodyweight exercises
- Day 12: Rest
- Day 13: 20-minute walk + 10 minutes of resistance band exercises
- Day 14: 25-minute jog + 10 minutes of bodyweight exercises

WEEK 3:

- Day 15: Rest
- Day 16: 30-minute bike ride + 10 minutes of resistance band exercises
- Day 17: 30-minute yoga session
- Day 18: 25-minute swim + 10 minutes of bodyweight exercises
- Day 19: Rest
- Day 20: 20-minute walk + 10 minutes of resistance band exercises
- Day 21: 30-minute jog + 10 minutes of bodyweight exercises

WEEK 4:

Day 22: Rest

Day 23: 25-minute jog + 10 minutes of resistance band exercises

Day 24: 30-minute yoga session

Day 25: 25-minute swim + 10 minutes of bodyweight exercises

Day 26: Rest

Day 27: 20-minute walk + 10 minutes of resistance band exercises

Day 28: 30-minute jog + 10 minutes of bodyweight exercises

Remember to gradually increase the intensity and duration of your workouts as your body adapts to the exercise routine.

In addition to exercise, it is important to fuel your body with the right nutrients to support weight gain. Be sure to consume enough calories and eat a balanced diet with plenty of protein, complex carbohydrates, and healthy fats.

Conclusion

As we reach the end of this high-calorie smoothie recipes book, I want to express my heartfelt gratitude for taking the time to explore these recipes with me. Whether you are looking to gain weight or simply enjoy a delicious and healthy treat, I hope that this book has provided you with valuable insights into the world of smoothie making.

In this journey, we have discovered the power of wholesome, high-calorie ingredients and the many benefits they offer. We have learned how to combine these ingredients in creative and delicious ways, using various techniques and kitchen tools to make the perfect smoothie.

But most importantly, we have learned that the path to healthy weight gain is not just about the food we consume, but also about the mindset we bring to the table. It is about embracing our bodies, listening to their needs, and treating them with love and respect.

As you continue on your journey to a healthier you, I encourage you to keep experimenting with these recipes and finding new ways to nourish your body. Remember to stay active, prioritize self-care, and above all, trust the journey.

Thank you once again for joining me on this adventure, and here's to a happy and healthy future filled with delicious, high-calorie smoothies!

FOR ANY QUESTIONS OR FURTHER ASSITANCE WITH REGARDS TO THE RECIPES IN THIS BOOK, CONTACT ME VIA EMAIL: iamgeorginatracy7@gmail.com. **I WILL BE GLAD TO ASSIST YOU.**